©Copyright Joan Lowery Nixon 1978

ISBN: 0-87973-378-0 Casebound
ISBN: 0-87973-358-6 Paperbound

Library of Congress Catalog Card Number: 78-56879

Published, printed and bound by
Our Sunday Visitor, Inc.
Noll Plaza
Huntington, Indiana 46750

When God SPEAKS

BY JOAN LOWERY NIXON

ILLUSTRATED BY JAMES McILRATH

Our Sunday Visitor, Inc.
Huntington, Indiana 46750

DISCARD

ST. MATTHEWS LIBRARY
HILLSBORO, ORE.

7519

"God spoke to Moses,"
the mother said. And the boy asked,
"Why doesn't God speak to me?"

The winds blew down from
around the mountaintop, whispering
cool and soft across the warm
meadow, touching
the boy's
face.

The boy lay on his stomach
and heard the quiet rustle
of field mice
scurrying through the long grass,
and the hum
of a fat bee burrowing
its head into the throat of
a wild trumpet flower.

The marsh birds rose
in a squawking cloud
from their hidden place
in the quivering reeds,
crying their songs
into the sun
as they skimmed over the lake.

G od talked to Moses
about what He wanted for His people,"
the mother said.
And the boy asked,
"Why doesn't God talk to me?"

He jumped to his feet
and ran barefoot through
the swishing grasses
to the water's edge. A startled
cricket chirped,
and a grasshopper
buzzed in a high arc
away from the
plop-plop of the boy's
hurrying feet.

Little waves from the lake
murmured up in icy curls
around the boy's toes,
slipping and hissing
bubbles of foam
on the wet shore.

Out on the lake
a fish jumped, splashing the water
with a slap,
and a sleek brown duck
rippled the surface
of the water
as he dived
after the fish.

God called to Moses
to come to the mountaintop,"
the mother said.
    And the boy asked,
"Why doesn't God call to me?"

High overhead a lone goose,
separated from its flock,
cried into the stillness;
and far in the distance
the call was returned.
Sun glinted from the goose's white
underbelly, as it banked
in its flight, crying
and flying toward the call.

ST. MATTHEWS LIBRARY
HILLSBORO, ORE

The dark pines
at the edge of the meadow
sighed as they swayed,
and somewhere
in the forest
a small bird twittered,
and a busy squirrel chattered.

The boy and his mother
walked along the shore of the
lake, their toes pressing
into the cool mud.

A small gray frog
croaked hoarsely as they passed,
and with a hop and a plop,
hid under the matted weeds
that clustered at the edge
of the water.

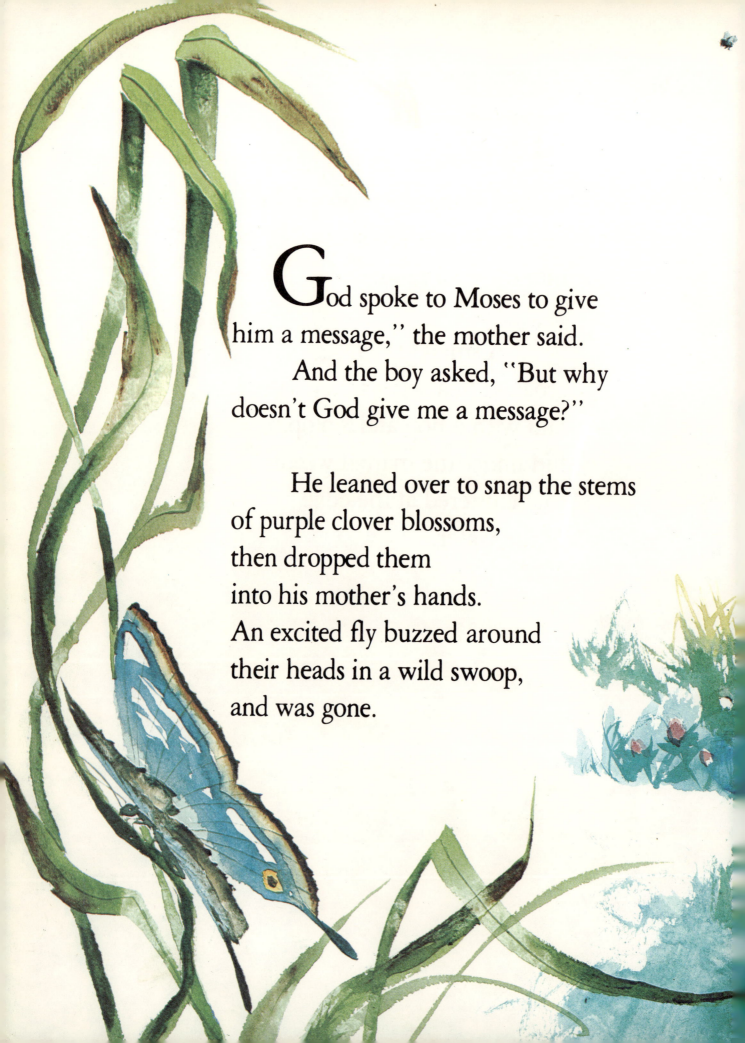

God spoke to Moses to give
him a message,'' the mother said.
      And the boy asked, ''But why
doesn't God give me a message?''

      He leaned over to snap the stems
of purple clover blossoms,
then dropped them
into his mother's hands.
An excited fly buzzed around
their heads in a wild swoop,
and was gone.

She tied
the clover stems
into a chain
and placed it
around her neck.

A hummingbird's swift wings
beat the air into slivers of whispers
before it darted across the meadow.
And somewhere in the forest
a twig cracked loudly.

God spoke to His people through Moses," the mother said.

And the boy asked, "But that was long ago. Why doesn't God speak now? Why doesn't He speak to me?"

"He does speak to you," the mother said. "You have to listen to hear Him."

She climbed on a large
flat rock; and the boy climbed up
beside her, resting his head
in her lap, feeling the
warmth from the rough
stone on his
back.

A thin stream
gurgled its way
around the rock,
losing itself
in the lake, and
somewhere overhead
a mockingbird trilled
a rush of clear notes.

"What does God say when He talks to me?" the boy asked his mother.

"He says, 'I love you,'" his mother answered.

"I haven't heard Him."

"There are other ways of saying 'I love you' besides using words," she said. "God has spoken to you today in many ways. Think about it and remember."

The boy thought,
and he listened.
And as he listened
he remembered what he had heard.
Then he smiled at his mother,
because he understood.

   The mother smoothed his damp
hair away from his forehead,
and hummed a soft tune
that melted into the sunlight.
The boy closed his eyes,
listening to God's words around him
until he fell asleep.